This Journal Belongs To:

_____

Vision Board & Inspirational Photos

Vision Board & Inspirational Photos

What Can I Do Today That My Future Self Will Thank Me For?

What Are My Short-Term Goals?

How Can I Grow In The Next 12 Months?

What Are My Most Important Values?

How Can I Add More Happiness To My Day?

What Am I Most Afraid Of?

What Would I Do If I Had 6 Months Left To Live?

Say Something Nice To Yourself.

What Are The Things I Love / Like About Myself?

What Will You Do If You Had A Million Dollars?

What Are You Passionate About?

How Would You Describe Yourself?

Do You Love Yourself? Why or Why Not? How Can You Love Yourself More Today?

What Are Your Biggest Goals And Dreams?

What Are The Top 5 Destinations You Wish To Visit? Why?

Who Are The People That Inspire You? Why?

What Are The Top 5 Books You'd Like To Read? Why?

If You Are To Die Tomorrow, What Would Your Biggest Regret Be?

What Do You Like To Do For Fun?

What Do You Do When You Feel Down? Is It Ok To Cry? Is It Ok To Shout? How Do You Let Your Frustrations Out?

What Do You Do When You Feel So Much Stress?

What Kept You Busy Today?

What Opportunities Are You Looking For?

What Are The Most Important Things You've Learned In Life So Far?

If You Had An Hour Left To Live, What Would You Do?

What Makes You Unique?

What Accomplishment Are You Most Proud Of?

What Are Your Strengths?

What Are Your Weaknesses?

What Do You Do When People Don't Seem To Like You?

What Advice Would You Give To Yourself 5 Years Ago?

Where Do You Feel Safest?

What Is Your Happiest Memory?

What Do You Wish Your Parents Knew About You?

What Does Failure Mean To You?

What Are You Ashamed Of?

What Are Your Long-Term Goals? How Do You Plan To Achieve It?

www.ingramcontent.com/pod-product-compliance
Lightning Source LLC
Chambersburg PA
CBHW071324080526
44587CB00018B/3344